Quotes
to Start
the Day

by
Susan
Savion

Incentive Publications, Inc.
Nashville, Tennessee

Dedicated to the students of Clary Middle School, Syracuse, New York

Design and Illustrations by Kathleen Bullock
Cover by Robert Voigts
Edited by Jodie Fransen and Marjorie Frank

ISBN 978-0-86530-422-2

1   2   3   4   5   6   7   8   9   10   13   12   11   10

Printed by Sheridan Books, Inc., Chelsea, Michigan • March 2010
www.incentivepublications.com

CONTENTS

	Quotes and Activities	Page

Start the Day Off Right!

An interesting quote is a spark to ignite your mind! The 55 quotes in this book are specifically chosen to wake up the brain and inspire, delight, or puzzle students enough to engage them with an important idea to carry through the day. The collection includes wise, witty, inspiring, curious, and insightful quotes. Each can challenge students to reflect, relate an idea to their own lives, and share their ideas with others. Of course, the quotes don't have to start the day or class period. You can use them in any setting where you'd like to light a spark for students.

As You Use the Quotes . . .

- Introduce students to the idea of aphorisms, adages, and proverbs. Ask them to find definitions of these words and share examples.

- The main purpose of this book is to get students to engage with the quote. So, be sure to encourage them to give opinions about it, relate it to their own experience, and ponder how the ideas or advice might be useful or applicable throughout the day. We know from brain research that learners internalize information by actively processing it and relating it to prior knowledge.

- We also know from brain research that emotions drive attention, meaning, and memory. So allow students to express fear, opposition, delight, sadness, joy, or humor that is triggered by these quotes.

- Make sure students have a chance to share their reflections about the quote.

- Share your own responses to the quotes. Take part in the activities. Consult the Teacher Notes on pages 62–64 to find additional information or activities for each quote.

- When possible, give students an opportunity to learn more about the speakers (or writers) of the quotes. Learn about the place and time in which that person lived, the influence on others, and the passions and beliefs.

- Many quotes, particularly those from the past, use the word "man" or "men" or masculine pronouns. Remind students that the idea applies to all humans.

- Don't forget about a quote after the activity is done. Keep quotes posted on the wall for a while. Refer to them. Ask students how a quote from past weeks is affecting them now.

Different Ways to Use the Quotes

Start the class period, session, or class by reading the quote to students. Also project the quote, place the quote on the board or on a poster, or give a copy to each student. Introduce the quote, and make sure all the words are understood before students begin other engagement with the quote.

Then, use any of these approaches:

● Use a quote as a short inspiration. Read it aloud, show it to students, and take a few minutes for students to respond and react.

● Use the quote and the activity page as a short warm-up activity. Students can do one, some, or all of the items on the page.

● Use the quote as a springboard for a longer lesson. Most of the pages can be extended to include discussion and sharing of students' written responses.

Topics Covered in the Quotes

Topics	Quotes	Topics	Quotes	Topics	Quotes
Accomplishment	1, 10, 17, 24, 27, 30, 42, 51, 53	Hate	49	Risk-taking	6, 22, 30, 47
Ambition	1, 6, 27, 42	Inner resources	2, 4	Sacrifice	10
Attitude	5, 7, 15, 17, 20, 22, 25, 44, 55	Lateness	45	Self-determination	2, 38
Be yourself	2, 21, 33, 52	Love	8	Self-expression	28
Care for others	19, 46, 53, 54	Luck	42	Self-respect	11, 29
Character	23	Music	31	Speaking	36
Courage	5, 6, 11, 30, 47, 48, 51	Nature	9	Success	17, 27
Do the right thing	34	Persistence	18, 27, 30, 42	Talents	33
Enthusiasm	55	Popularity	34, 41	Temper	12
Expectations	17, 40	Possibilities	2, 5, 6, 9, 16, 22, 26, 47	Tongue	32
Failure	18, 37, 43	Reading, books	3, 13, 39	Trustworthiness	35
Good beginnings	50	Resilience	2, 28, 37	Waiting	14

1

"Even if you're on the right track, you'll get run over if you just sit there."

– Will Rogers

● Explain the metaphor in this quote by putting Will Rogers' advice into your own words.

_____

_____

_____

● A popular idiom warns us not to "rest on our laurels." This saying uses an old symbol to make a point. (A laurel wreath would be placed on the head of any Olympic winner in ancient Greece and Rome.) Compare this idiom about winning to the words by Will Rogers.

_____

_____

_____

● Describe a situation that shows Will's statement to be true.

_____

_____

Will Rogers (1879–1935) *was a cowboy movie star who became known not only for his amazing roping skills, but also for his wisecracks and humorous observations about life. This philosopher, who never finished high school, never stopped learning. Born on a Cherokee Nation ranch in Oklahoma, he went on to become a popular broadcaster, Broadway and movie star (in 71 movies), and writer of more than 4,000 syndicated newspaper columns. He also wrote six books.*

 Quotes to Start the Day

2

"...it does not matter where you came from, or who your parents were. What counts is who you are."

– Barbara Jordan

● What do you think Barbara Jordan means by the phrase "who you are"?

_____

_____

_____

● Do you agree or disagree with this quote? Explain your choice.

_____

_____

● Describe a time when you have seen someone judged by who their parents are, where they live, or some factor in their background.

_____

_____

● How would you explain who you are?

_____

_____

Barbara Jordan (1936–1996) *was the first black woman elected to the Texas Senate. For over thirty years, she wrote actively and spoke dynamically about the most critical issues facing Americans from all walks of life. In 1994, President Clinton awarded her the Presidential Medal of Freedom, the highest award to a civilian in the country.*

8

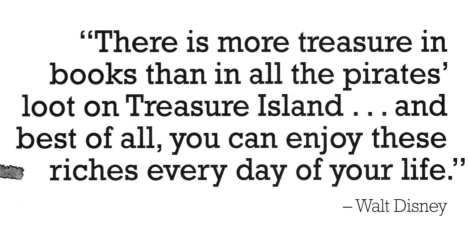

"There is more treasure in books than in all the pirates' loot on Treasure Island . . . and best of all, you can enjoy these riches every day of your life."

— Walt Disney

● What is the treasure to which Disney is referring?

_____

_____

_____

● Name a few books you have read that provided you with "riches."
In the second column, tell what "treasure" was found in each book.

Book Title	Treasure You Found

Walt Disney (1901–1966) *was an American cartoon artist, animator, showman, and film producer. The creator of Mickey Mouse and founder of the Disneyland® and Walt Disney World® Theme Parks, he produced the first animated film with sound,* **Steamboat Willie (1928)**, *and the first full-length animated feature,* **Snow White**, *in 1937. Walt Disney received more than 950 honors and citations from every nation in the world, including 48 Academy Awards® and seven Emmys® in his lifetime.*

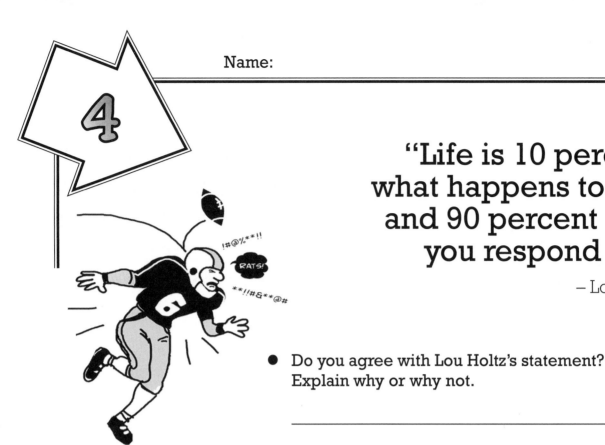

4

"Life is 10 percent what happens to you and 90 percent how you respond to it."

– Lou Holtz

● Do you agree with Lou Holtz's statement? Explain why or why not.

_____

_____

● Tell about something that happened to you and how you responded to it.

_____

_____

_____

● How might you have responded differently to the above situation and what difference would that have made?

_____

_____

_____

Lou Holtz (1937–) *went from being an undersized football player to one of the most successful college football coaches in history. He led six different college teams to bowl games, and was the only coach to have four different college programs ranked in the top 20. Holtz was admired for his sense of humor and his ability to inspire players, and was awarded the National Coach of the Year honor several times. After retiring, he went on to become a television commentator, football analyst, motivational speaker, and author. In 2008, Holtz was elected to the College Football Hall of Fame.*

10

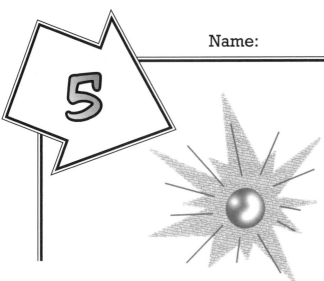

"The sun cannot shine into an inverted bowl."

– Chinese proverb

- Define *inverted*.

_____

- Explain this metaphor by putting the quote into your own words.

_____

_____

_____

- Other Chinese proverbs, including these, have a similar message:

"Be in readiness for favorable winds."

"A closed mind is like a closed book; just a block of wood."

"Teachers open the door. You enter by yourself."

In the space below, write your own proverb with a message about one of the following:

| opportunity | being open-minded | learning |
| luck | being prepared | fate |

(Remember that a proverb is a brief phrase expressing a basic truth that can be applied to everyday situations.)

_____

_____

_____

11

6

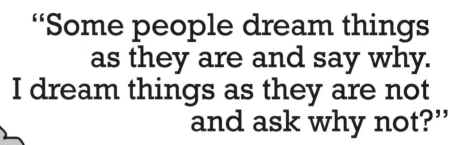

"Some people dream things as they are and say why. I dream things as they are not and ask why not?"

– George Bernard Shaw

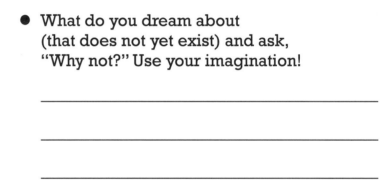

● What do you dream about (that does not yet exist) and ask, "Why not?" Use your imagination!

_____

_____

_____

● What are some things that exist today that you cannot imagine living without?

_____

_____

_____

_____

_____

George Bernard Shaw (1856–1950) *was a popular Irish playwright whose most well-known drama* **Pygmalion** *was the basis for the hit movie,* **My Fair Lady**. *He wrote plays, music, novels, and journalistic articles. He made many strong comments on social issues of the day (often with humor), and was especially passionate against exploitation of the working class.*

"If your house is on fire, warm yourself by it."

– Spanish proverb

● What message is common to the proverb and the haiku poem (below)?

_____

_____

_____

● Can you think of a time when something you thought was negative turned out to be positive? Explain.

The Great Chicago Fire of 1871

_____

_____

_____

● Work together with a partner to create a proverb, haiku poem, or other short poem with a similar message.

_____

_____

_____

"Since my house burned down I now have a better view of the rising moon."

– Masahide Haiku

13

"If you have love, you don't need to have anything else. If you don't have it, it doesn't matter what else you have."

– Sir James M. Barrie

● Discuss this quote with at least two other people. Of the three of you, how many agree that these statements are true?

_____

● Describe a situation that shows how love has sustained someone through a hard time.

_____

_____

_____

● Literature is filled with characters who are rich in worldly goods but do not have love in their lives. Can you name two (or more) such characters?

_____

_____

_____

Sir James M. Barrie (1860–1937) *is best known as the author of* **Peter Pan**, *the boy who refused to grow up. Barrie and his wife became the guardians of five boys when their parents died, and he based the characters in the* **Peter Pan** *story on these boys.*

Peter Pan, based on a drawing by the author, James Barrie

9

"To me every hour of the light and dark is a miracle. Every cubic inch of space is a miracle."

– Walt Whitman

● Name some things in your life or the natural world that are especially precious (miracles!) to you.

_____

_____

_____

● Think of a time when you felt glad to be alive, experiencing the excitement that Whitman expressed in his quote. Tell where you were and what you were doing or seeing (or smelling, feeling, touching, hearing).

_____

_____

_____

_____

Walt Whitman (1819–1892) *is considered to be one of America's greatest poets. Born on Long Island, New York, he was a teacher and a newspaperman before publishing his first book of poems titled* **Leaves of Grass**. *Many of his poems celebrated the freedom and dignity of the individual and sang the praises of democracy and the connection of all humans.*

"You have to set goals…and you have to make sacrifices to reach those goals."

– Sonja Henning

● List five goals for yourself. For each one, identify sacrifices you may have to make in order to achieve the goal.

Goal	Sacrifices

● Describe a time you reached a goal. How did it feel?

_____

_____

Sonja Henning (1969–) *was a standout on the Stanford University basketball team. After graduating with a degree in economics in 1991, she took a year to play professional ball in Sweden, and then decided to pursue a law degree at Duke University. For nine years, she worked at practicing law and playing women's pro basketball, first with the ABL and then with the WNBA. She retired from basketball in 2004 and continues to serve her community as a lawyer, businesswoman, and activist.*

16

"It takes a great deal of courage to stand up to your enemies, but even more to stand up to your friends."

– J. K. Rowling

- Think of a time when you had to stand up to an enemy. What happened?

EVEN A MAGIC WAND CAN'T GIVE ME THE COURAGE TO CONFRONT MY FRIENDS.

_____

_____

_____

- Now think of a time when you had to stand up to a friend. What happened?

_____

_____

- Based on your own experiences, do you agree with J. K. Rowling's quote? Explain your choice.

_____

_____

_____

J. K. Rowling (1965–) *is the famous British author who created the* **Harry Potter** *series. She began writing fantasy stories when she was a child. Most of her writing on that first Harry Potter book was done in cafes, where she walked with her baby who slept while she wrote. The book was rejected by 12 publishers. Now, there are multiple* **Harry Potter** *novels and movies. Ms. Rowling has gone from being on welfare to being a multimillionaire and one of the most recognized authors in the world.*

"If you lose your temper, you've lost the argument."

— English proverb

"Temper is a weapon that we hold by the blade."
— Sir James M. Barrie

"The worst-tempered people I've ever met were the people who knew they were wrong."
— Wilson Mizner

"A quick temper will make a fool of you soon enough."
— Bruce Lee

"The best remedy for a short temper is a long walk."
— Joseph Joubert

"The one who cannot restrain their anger will wish undone, what their temper and irritation prompted them to do."
— Horace

● Make an X by the statements above that seem to you to be true.

● What have you done in anger that you wish you could undo?

_____

● What do you do when you feel your temper flaring? What advice could you give to others about how to control their temper?

_____

_____

_____

The next time you feel your temper rising, go for a walk—and see if that helps, as Joseph Joubert believes it will.

13

"When I get a little money, I buy books; and if any is left, I buy food and clothes."

– Erasmus

- The thirst for knowledge and for stories is a basic human desire. Some might even call this a "need." Do you agree that this is a need?

_____

- Why might books be more important to someone than the other essentials of life?

_____

_____

- Finish the statement for yourself:

When I get a little money, I buy _____; and if

any is left, I buy _____ and _____.

- Share your responses with a partner and defend your choices.

Erasmus (1466–1536) _was a Dutch writer, scholar, teacher, and speaker. He moved from city to city working as a tutor and lecturer, constantly writing and searching out ancient manuscripts. More than 1,500 of his letters survive. His **Adages** (a collection of 1,500 Latin proverbs) established his scholarly reputation. Most of his other early works attacked corrupt church practices. He fought and wrote against ignorance and superstition._

19

14

"Good things come to those who wait."

– American proverb

"All good things arrive unto them that wait—and don't die in the meantime."

– Mark Twain

"Everything comes to him who hustles while he waits."

– Thomas A. Edison

I'M STILL WAITING!

● Which of these quotes is your favorite? Why?

_____

_____

_____

● What is something you had to wait for? Was it worth the wait? Why or why not?

_____

_____

_____

Thomas Edison (1847–1931) *was one of the most prolific inventors in world history. He received more than 1,000 patents for his innovations, which include the workable electric light bulb, phonograph, and motion picture camera.*

Mark Twain (1835–1910), *whose real name was Samuel Clemens, was a great author and humorist. His wise and witty sayings have made him one of the most quoted American authors.*

15

"What we see depends mainly on what we look for."

– John Lubbock

● Many people miss seeing things that are right
before their eyes, usually because they weren't
actively looking for them. Right now, try to describe
everything that is outside the front of your school.

_____

_____

_____

● This principle applies to the way we see people, too. Choose a person in
whom you usually see something "negative" and write down a "positive"
quality you know is there or will look for in this person the next time you
see him or her. Write the person's name and the positive quality. (Do not
use the real name. Choose a fictitious name instead.)

Sir John Lubbock (1834–1913) *spent his life in
constant search for knowledge. Born in London,
England, he was fortunate to receive a good
education. He went on to become a renowned
archaeologist, biologist, and politician.
Through his scientific
discoveries and
textbooks, he made
major contributions
to education. He
challenged people
to better themselves
and to help
better society.*

_____

_____

_____

_____

_____

_____

         Quotes to Start the Day

16

WOW!

"When I look into the future, it's so bright it burns my eyes."

– Oprah Winfrey

● Take a quick survey of five people (including yourself). Ask them to name something they see as a "bright" possibility in their future. List the most interesting survey results here.

1. _____

2. _____

3. _____

4. _____

5. _____

● Winfrey uses hyperbole in her metaphor about the future. Create your own positive statement that is also an exaggerated way of expressing your vision for the future by finishing the sentence:

When I look into the future, it's so _____

_____

_____

Oprah Winfrey (1954–) *is a billionaire and one of the best-known women in the world. Born in Mississippi, she overcame childhood difficulties to become a broadcaster, Academy Award-nominated actor, talk show host, activist, and philanthropist. In 1998, she received a Lifetime Achievement Award from the National Academy of Television Arts and Sciences, and Time Magazine went on to name her one of the 100 Most Influential People of the 20th Century.*

17

"You have to expect things of yourself before you can do them."

– Michael Jordan

- Name four things that you expect of yourself.

  _____

  _____

- Do you agree or disagree with Michael Jordan's statement? Explain your choice.

  _____

  _____

  _____

  _____

- How does it make a difference that Michael Jordan is the person speaking in this quote?

  _____

  _____

  _____

*Many people call **Michael Jordan (1963–)** "the greatest basketball player of all time." He led the University of North Carolina to a national championship in 1982, and went on to win six NBA championships, five MVP awards, and two Olympic gold medals. His stunts and leaping ability earned him the nicknames "Air Jordan" and "His Air-ness." Since retiring as a player, Jordan has gone on to many successful business ventures, including endorsement of Nike's most popular basketball shoe. He was elected to the Basketball Hall of Fame in 2009.*

18

"Our greatest glory consists not in never falling, but in rising every time we fall."

– Oliver Goldsmith

IT'S NOT THE FALLING SO MUCH - IT'S THE GETTING UP!

● Tell about a time when you "fell" and DID get back up and try again.

_____

_____

● Who else have you known, read about, or seen that got up again after "falling" or failing?

_____

● Comment on one of these quotes. (Tell what you think about it.)

"I honestly think it is better to be a failure at something you love than to be a success at something you hate." **– George Burns**

In spite of many personal failures, **Oliver Goldsmith (1730–1774)** *became a successful writer, poet, and physician. Known for his novel* **The Vicar of Wakefield** *and his ironic poem, "An Elegy on the Death of a Mad Dog," he also wrote plays and a classic children's story,* **The History of Little Goody Two-Shoes**. *For many years, he published a series of letters titled* **The Citizen of the World**, *in which he used a fictional visitor to England to give commentary on British society.*

"I've failed over and over and over again in my life and that is why I succeed."
– Michael Jordan

_____

_____

_____

_____

_____

19

"A candle loses nothing of its light by lighting another candle."

– Father James Keller

● Explain the metaphor of the candle.

_____

_____

● Tell about a time when you helped another person.

_____

_____

_____

● In the above situation, did you feel diminished, the same, or improved? Describe your feelings.

_____

_____

Father James Keller (1900–1977), *a Catholic priest, was a public figure, a radio and television personality, a writer and editor, and a religious leader. He founded a movement called "The Christophers," which taught that every person has something to give to the world. His own motto was a Chinese proverb: "It's better to light one candle than to curse the darkness."*

● Sketch a simple drawing of some way that a person could "light someone else's candle" in the way it is meant by the writer, Father James Keller.

20

"...it's better to be a hopeful person than a cynical, grumpy one, because you have to live in the same world either way, and if you're hopeful, you have more fun."

– Barbara Kingsolver

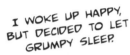

I WOKE UP HAPPY, BUT DECIDED TO LET GRUMPY SLEEP.

● Define *cynical*.

_____

_____

● How could being hopeful lead to having more fun?

_____

_____

● Think about yourself in the categories that Barbara Kingsolver has mentioned (cynical and grumpy or hopeful). Make an X on the continuum line to show where you fall in this relationship of cynical to hopeful:

cynical   hopeful

● How do you think the illustration above relates to the quote?

_____

_____

_____

_____

Barbara Kingsolver (1955–) *is a best-selling novelist, short story writer, poet, and nonfiction writer. Her many popular and prize-winning books include* **The Bean Trees**, **Animal Dreams**, **Pigs in Heaven**, *and* **The Poisonwood Bible**. *Kingsolver creates memorable characters and through them, reflects keen insights into human nature.*

26

21

"The shoe that fits one person pinches another . . ."

– Carl Jung

I WOULDN'T WANT TO BE IN YOUR SHOES!

HE SHOULD TRY WALKING A MILE IN MY SHOES.

● Explain the metaphor in Jung's quote.

_____

_____

● What "shoe" that fits you might pinch someone else?

_____

_____

_____

● What "shoe" that fits someone else might pinch you?

_____

_____

_____

Carl Gustav Jung (1875–1961) *was a Swiss-German psychoanalyst who investigated dreams and developed several theories of the unconscious. He used the technique of free association and explained human behavior as a combination of four psychic functions: thinking, feeling, intuition, and sensation. He also coined the term "synchronicity" to describe life's "meaningful coincidences."*

Name: _____

22

BaH-HUMbUg! / Hot-dog!

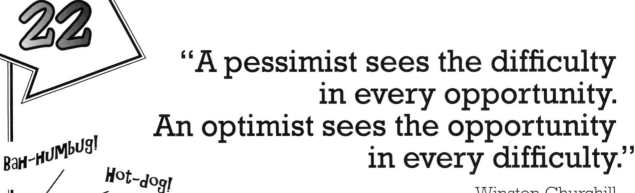

"A pessimist sees the difficulty
in every opportunity.
An optimist sees the opportunity
in every difficulty."

– Winston Churchill

● For each situation below, tell how a pessimist might see it.
Then tell how an optimist might see it.

A student studied hard for a test, got to the test, and was totally baffled by the questions—ending with a poor grade.

A pessimist might _____

_____

_____

An optimist might _____

_____

_____

A kid who plays drums loves music, and always wanted to be in a band learns that a local teen band is looking for a new drummer.

A pessimist might _____

_____

_____

An optimist might _____

_____

_____

● Do you consider yourself mostly
an optimist or a pessimist?

_____

Explain your answer.

_____

_____

_____

Winston Churchill (1874–1965) *is best known as the leader of Great Britain during World War II. He was also an orator, artist, and writer. His words and examples have been motivating people for more than a half century.*

"Our character is what we do when we think no one is looking."

– Abraham Lincoln

● Do you think most people do the same thing when someone is looking as they would do when someone is not?

_____

● What is something you do when no one is looking that shows your character?

_____

_____

● Describe an action that you know about which was done by someone who believed no one was looking—an action that shows something about the person's character. (This "someone" may be you, someone you know, or a stranger you saw or heard about. Don't use any real names.)

_____

_____

_____

Abraham Lincoln (1809–1865), *the 16th U.S. president, was in office from 1861 until his assassination in 1865. During most of that time, the Civil War raged. The spirit that guided Lincoln was this (from his Second Inaugural Address, now inscribed on one wall of the Lincoln Memorial in Washington, D.C.): "With malice toward none; with charity for all...let us strive on to finish the work we are in; to bind up the nation's wounds..."*

● What does Lincoln's statement imply about integrity?

_____

_____

_____

"You can get all A's and still flunk life."

– Walker Percy

● List some things that come to your mind when you read the phrase "flunk life."

I GOT MY 'A'. NOW WHAT?

_____

_____

_____

_____

● In what ways do you think the habits you develop in school affect your life later on?

_____

_____

_____

● What is one thing you intend to do that will keep you from "flunking life?"

_____

_____

Walker Percy (1916–1990) was an American author of novels and nonfiction works. After earning a medical degree, Percy spent several years recovering from tuberculosis. During that time, he did a lot of reading—and decided that he would write and study about sickness of "the soul" rather than sickness of the body. Percy published several successful novels that explored how and why people felt "dislocated" in modern life. These include **The Moviegoer**, **Love in the Ruins**, **The Last Gentleman**, and **The Second Coming**.

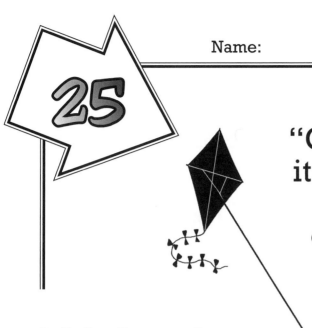

25

"Children must know that it is not their aptitude but their attitude that will determine their altitude."

– Jesse Jackson

● Define these words:

aptitude _____

attitude _____

altitude _____

● Explain Jackson's quote in your own words.

_____

_____

● Describe someone you know who has a lot of potential but whose attitude keeps him or her from being all they could be. (Do not use any real names.)

_____

_____

Reverend Jesse Jackson (1941–), *sometimes called "The Conscience of the Nation," graduated from the public schools in Greenville, South Carolina, and went to college on a football scholarship. He went on to work full-time in the civil rights movement, challenging Americans to be inclusive and to establish priorities for the benefit of all. As founder of the Rainbow/PUSH Coalition, he is known for bringing people together in spite of differences in race, culture, class, gender, and religious belief. He is also known for challenging children to do their best and take education seriously.*

26

"Everyone has inside of him a piece of good news. The good news is that you don't know how great you can be! How much you can love! What you can accomplish! And what your potential is!"

– Anne Frank

- Do you agree with what Anne Frank is saying in this quote?

_____

- Explain your answer.

_____

_____

_____

- What do YOU intend to accomplish?

_____

_____

Anne Frank (1929–1945), a German-Jewish girl, wrote a diary while hiding from the Nazis during World War II. For over two years, Anne and her family lived secretly in an attic above her father's place of business. In 1944, the family was betrayed and arrested. Anne died in the Nazi concentration camp at Bergen-Belsen in March of 1945. Her diary was later found and given to her father, who published it in 1947 as a message to young people about the dangers of hatred and prejudice.

- Given what you know and can find out about Anne Frank and the setting in which she wrote her diary, what can you infer about her from this one quote?

_____

_____

_____

_____

27

"The sleeping fox catches no poultry."

– Ben Franklin

● **What is *poultry*?**

_____

_____

● **Explain the proverb.**

_____

_____

● Benjamin Franklin wrote more than 700 proverbs and aphorisms (witty sayings). Here are the beginnings of a few. Finish them in your own way to give a message.

A bird in the hand is worth _____ .

You can lead a horse to water, but _____ .

He who hesitates is _____ .

Fools rush in where _____ .

_____ while the iron is hot.

Meanness is the parent of _____ .

Friendship cannot live without _____ .

Benjamin Franklin (1706–1790) *was America's best-known scientist, inventor, musician, chess player, diplomat, writer, and business strategist during his 84-year lifetime. By flying a kite, he proved that lightning is electricity. He also invented bifocal glasses and clean-burning stoves. As a statesman, he proposed plans for uniting the colonies. Through* **Poor Richard's Almanack** *and other writings—often in the form of proverbs—he spread many timeless, thought-provoking (and often humorous) insights and bits of advice. He was a strong voice for tolerance.*

28

HEAR ME ROAR!

"When you have a voice, you can speak about anything in the world with your own feelings and your own emotions."
– Jackie Warren Moore

● What do you think Jackie Moore means by the phrase "have a voice"?

_____

_____

● What is the one thing you would most like to speak about with your own voice?

_____

● What are some things you could do to help another person speak in his or her own voice?

_____

_____

● Name a person to whose voice you always pay attention. Explain your answer.

_____

_____

_____

_____

Jackie Warren Moore (1953–) *is a nationally recognized African-American poet, playwright, columnist, and theatrical director. She received the 1989 Unsung Heroine Award for Feminist Writing from the National Organization for Women. She has been honored for her community service—which has included helping students whose lives are caught up in gangs, weapons, and violence to use the "tool of poetry" to develop a voice of their own.*

34

29

"He that respects himself is safe from others: He wears a coat of mail that none can pierce."

– Henry Wadsworth Longfellow

- What was the original purpose of a coat of mail?

  _____

  _____

  _____

- Draw a cartoon that depicts the idea in Longfellow's statement.

  _____

  _____

  _____

- Describe what it means for you to "respect yourself." Use specific examples of what your self-respect would look like to someone else.

  _____

  _____

Henry Wadsworth Longfellow (1807–1882) was a great American poet. He is well remembered for his lyric poems that told stories and legends; two of his most famous are "Paul Revere's Ride" and "The Song of Hiawatha."

30

"You must do the thing you think you cannot do."

– Eleanor Roosevelt

● Name some things you think you cannot do.

_____

_____

● Why do you think Eleanor Roosevelt believes this?

_____

_____

_____

● Did you ever do something that you were afraid to attempt at first? If so, tell what it was and tell how you felt after you did it or tried it.

_____

_____

_____

_____

Eleanor Roosevelt (1884–1962) *was one of America's most influential First Ladies. She worked for social justice and blazed trails for women. She was the first woman to speak in front of a national convention, to write a syndicated column, to earn money as a lecturer, to be a radio commentator, and to hold regular press conferences. After raising six children with her husband Franklin Roosevelt, she turned her energies to a variety of reform movements including abolishing child labor, promoting civil rights, and establishing a minimum wage.*

31

"Music is a healing force ... all living spirits sing!"

– Joanne Shenandoah

- What kind of music is most healing or calming for you? (Tell why. Name some specific songs, if you wish.)

  _____

  _____

  _____

  _____

- Ask the same question (above) of five other people. Summarize what you learned from your survey.

  _____

  _____

- What evidence do you see that "all living spirits sing"? (Include yourself as a "living spirit.")

  _____

  _____

Joanne Shenandoah (1958–), _whose name means "She Sings" in her native language, is a member of the Wolf Clan of the Oneida Nation of Native Americans. She is a singer, composer, and guitarist who has recorded many albums and won many awards, including a Grammy Award. Joanne's original compositions use a blend of traditional and contemporary instruments to embellish the ancient songs of the Iroquois. Her music reflects a Native American philosophy and culture that continue to have a profound effect on the world today._

"Even four horses cannot pull back what the tongue has let go."

– Slovakian proverb

● **What does this proverb mean to you?**

_____

_____

● **Where have you seen proof that this proverb is true?**

_____

_____

_____

● **What message do all the proverbs below have in common with the Slovakian proverb (above)?**

_____

"Better a snake's tongue to sting you than a man's."
– Greek proverb

"Keep not two tongues in one mouth."
– Danish proverb

"The tongue slays quicker than the sword."
– Turkish proverb

"A word once out flies everywhere."
– French proverb

"Words have long tails."
– English proverb

33

> "Use the talents you possess, for the woods would be very silent if no birds sang except the best."
>
> – Henry Van Dyke

● List some of the talents that you possess.

_____   _____

_____   _____

_____   _____

_____   _____

● Write a 1 by the things (above) that you are very good at doing. Write a 2 by the talents that are not your best, but you use anyway. Write a 3 by those that you shy away from doing because you feel you are not good enough.

● Write one real-life example to explain Van Dyke's metaphor.

_____

_____

_____

Henry Van Dyke (1852–1933) *was an American clergyman, educator, and author, as well as pastor of a Presbyterian church in New York City and a professor of English literature at Princeton University. He was also U.S. minister to the Netherlands. Van Dyke wrote two popular Christmas stories,* **The First Christmas Tree** *and* **The Other Wise Man**. *He also wrote essays, poems, and lyrics for hymns.*

"What is popular is not always right; what is right is not always popular!"

– Hipparchus

● Identify something that is popular but not necessarily right.

_____

_____

● Identify something right that is not popular.

_____

_____

● Meet with a small group of students. Discuss this question: "Is it better to do something that is right or something that is popular?" Try to agree on an answer.

Write your group's answer and reasoning here:

_____

_____

_____

_____

_____

Hipparchus (190–220 B.C.) *was a Greek mathematician and astronomer who compiled the world's first star catalog. He is best known for his calculations on the rotation of Earth and attempts to calculate the length of a year. His image appears on coins minted under five different Roman emperors between A.D. 138 and A.D. 253.*

"Dogs are better than human beings because they know but do not tell."

– Emily Dickinson

- **What is your first response to this quote?**

  _____

  _____

- **Do you believe it would be a good thing for human beings to "know" but "not tell"?**

  _____

  Tell why or why not.

  _____

- **Dickinson's statement compares dogs and human beings. Create your own comparisons by finishing the sentences:**

  Dogs are better than human beings because _____

  _____

  Human beings are better than dogs because _____

  _____

Emily Dickinson (1830–1886) *is considered among the greatest of American poets. She wrote more than 1,800 poems of great emotional depth—most of them from the seclusion of her home. Many of her verses were about loss and death and mortality. Her imagery and metaphors come from both an acute observation of nature and a powerful imagination.*

36

"Be sincere; be brief; be seated."

– Franklin D. Roosevelt

● **What is wise about this advice?**

_____

_____

_____

● **Think of three situations where you (or someone else) could apply this advice.**

1. _____

2. _____

3. _____

● **Think of a situation in which you felt someone really wanted or needed your advice. Write it below, and then give your advice in the same style that F.D.R. used above.**

Situation I Chose:

Advice (Keep it concise!):

> **Franklin D. Roosevelt (1882–1945)** *was the 32nd president of the U.S. He won four elections, serving more terms than any other United States president. F.D.R. was crippled by polio, but became president and led the country out of the Great Depression and through most of World War II. He was an eloquent and inspiring speaker.*

37

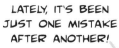

LATELY, IT'S BEEN JUST ONE MISTAKE AFTER ANOTHER!

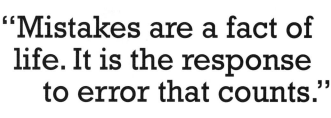

"Mistakes are a fact of life. It is the response to error that counts."

– Nikki Giovanni

List mistakes that you have made or that you have seen others make.	For each mistake, tell two or three different ways someone could respond.
	1 2 3
	1 2 3
	1 2 3
	1 2 3

Nikki Giovanni (1943–) *is an American poet, essayist, and lecturer, whose work reflects her pride in her African-American heritage. Her earliest collections of poetry, including* **Black Feeling** *and* **Black Talk***, capture the attitude of the civil rights movement. She has written not only about racism, the black power movement, feminism, and police brutality, but also about love, longing and loneliness. She also speaks out against hatred and violence.*

43

"He who claps his hands for the fool to dance is no better than the fool."

– African proverb

- In your own words, tell what this proverb means.

_____

_____

- Give two examples of a person who "claps his (or her) hands for the fool to dance." Explain the situation in which this happens. (Do not name any real names.)

  1. _____

  2. _____

- How would you illustrate this proverb?

  Draw it or describe an illustration that would be fitting.

    44

"Books can be dangerous. The best ones should be labeled 'This could change your life.'"

– Helen Exley

● This is an example of a "tongue in cheek" statement. Helen Exley was being a bit satirical, but wholly truthful. Explain the "danger" that this quote is "warning" about.

_____

_____

_____

● How could reading a book change someone's life?

_____

_____

_____

● Name a book you have read that has changed you in some way. Explain your choice.

_____

_____

_____

_____

_____

_____

Helen Exley (1966–) *creates gift books for children and young adults. She has worked with a team of staff members to collect, edit, and publish over 200 books containing hundreds of quotations for adults, children, and young adults. A few of her book titles are* **Wisdom for Our Times**, **Utterly Adorable Cats**, **Go Girl**, *and* **Me and My Friend**.

"Expecting the world to treat you fairly because you are good is like expecting the bull not to charge because you are a vegetarian."

– Dennis Wholey

● What is your response to this statement by Dennis Wholey?

_____

_____

I'M NOT AFRAID. I HAD TOFU FOR LUNCH!

● This quote is a simile—a type of metaphor that compares two unlike things using the word "like." Use your creativity to finish the metaphors below. Make sure you use a comparison of things that ordinarily would not be seen as the same.

A. Planning to get a good grade on a test when you didn't

bother to study is like _____

_____

B. Being betrayed by a friend is like _____

_____

C. Expecting _____

_____ is like asking a mouse to waltz with a walrus.

Dennis Wholey (1939–) *is a television host (**This is America**) and producer. He has written best-selling self-help books. His own struggles with alcohol and drugs have led him to focus his energies on trying to give hope and help to people who need change in their lives.*

41

"Anyone who is popular is bound to be disliked."

—Yogi Berra

● How is this statement contradictory?

_____

_____

_____

Yogi-isms

"A nickel ain't worth a dime anymore."

"I'm not going to buy my kids an encyclopedia. Let them walk to school like I did."

"I think Little League is wonderful. It keeps the kids out of the house."

"When you come to a fork in the road, take it."

● How can a person be popular and disliked at the same time?

_____

_____

_____

● Do you know a popular person who is also disliked? Without naming any real names, tell why the person is disliked.

_____

_____

_____

Yogi Berra (1925–) *is an American hero. A baseball Hall-of-Famer, he played for the New York Yankees for 17 seasons and was famous for swinging at and hitting seemingly impossible pitches. Later, he went on to manage the Yankees and the New York Mets, and to coach the Houston Astros. Yogi was as famous for his cheerful personality as for his baseball talent. He constantly spoke in aphorisms (known as "Yogi-isms")—that have made him the most quoted personality of recent history.*

42

"I find that the harder I work, the more luck I seem to have."

– Thomas Jefferson

Monticello, Jefferson's home

● What do you think about Jefferson's connection between work and luck?

_____

_____

● Someone else said this:

"I've found that luck is quite predictable. If you want more luck, take more chances. Be more active. Show up more often."
– Unknown

● What do you think this speaker meant by "Show up more often"?

_____

_____

_____

Thomas Jefferson (1743–1826), *was the third U.S. president and author of the* **Declaration of Independence.** *He was one of the founders of the United States and a fervent defender of liberty. He also donated his own large collection of books to establish the Library of Congress. He was an inventor, architect, horticulturalist, statesman, and linguist. Jefferson wished to be remembered for three interrelated causes: freedom from Britain, freedom of conscience, and freedom maintained through education.*

43

"A man can fail many times, but he isn't a failure until he begins to blame someone else."

– John Burroughs

● Describe a situation in which you have seen this happen: someone fails at something and finds someone else to blame. (The someone could be you. Don't use any real names.)

_____

_____

_____

Thomas Edison, John Burroughs, Henry Ford

● Why do you think people blame others when they fail?

_____

_____

_____

● What is an alternative to blaming someone else when you fail?

_____

_____

_____

John Burroughs (1837–1921) *was an American naturalist (and avid fisherman) who was an important part of the beginnings of the conservation movement in the United States. He was a popular and prolific essayist who wrote about the natural world. He wrote over 30 books and hundreds of essays that came out of his trips into the wilderness.*

44

"...the meaning of things lies not in the things themselves, but in our attitude towards them."

– Antoine de Saint-Exupéry

• Brandy is passionately loyal to her friends, works hard at being a good friend, and hopes to keep her friends forever. Malika says, "Friends are a dime a dozen. You can always get new ones when you tire of your old ones." How do you think the meaning of friendship differs for the two girls?

_____

_____

• Write a short explanation of the meaning (for you) of these items:

		Its Meaning for YOU
1	popularity	
2	your family	
3	money	

Reread what you wrote. Discuss with someone how your attitude toward each thing is reflected in what you believe the meaning to be.

Antoine de Saint-Exupéry (1900–1944) *is the French author, thinker, mechanic, and pilot best known for his fable,* **Le Petit Prince** **(The Little Prince)**. *This book is said to be the third most read book in the world (after* **The Bible** *and* **The Koran**). *During his flights in the French Air Force, he thought about such things as the meaning of life, liberty, solitude, and friendship. He published his reflections, and his books were an immediate success.*

45

"Better late than never."

– English proverb

"A little too late is much too late."

– German proverb

- Survey at least ten people. Ask them which of the above quotes is closest to what they believe about being late or having something happen late. Write your results here:

  _____   _____

  German proverb   English proverb

- Which proverb would you choose? Explain why.

  _____

  _____

- Describe a situation from your experience in which one or the other of the proverbs proved to be true.

  _____

  _____

- Write your own original proverb about being late.

  _____

46

Charles Dickens

"No one is useless in this world who lightens the burdens of another."

– Charles Dickens

● List two ways you could literally "lighten a burden" for someone.

_____

_____

● List four ways you could metaphorically "lighten a burden" for someone.

1. _____

2. _____

3. _____

4. _____

● Join with a partner. Share your lists. Circle everything on your list above that was also on your partner's list.

● With your partner, come up with two more ideas (one literal and one metaphorical) that were not on either of your lists.

_____

_____

Charles Dickens (1812–1870) *is one of the most popular novelists in history. He wrote during the Victorian era in England, cleverly pointing out the social ills of the times. He created fascinating characters and used wonderful metaphors, rhythm, and suspense. Some of his best-known books are* **A Christmas Carol**, **A Tale of Two Cities**, **Oliver Twist**, *and* **Great Expectations**. *Dickens had great care and concern for the poor, the suffering, and the oppressed in his society.*

52

47

"Twenty years from now you will be more disappointed by the things that you didn't do than by the ones you did do. So throw off the bowlines. Sail away from the safe harbor. Catch the trade winds in your sails. Explore. Dream. Discover."

– Mark Twain

- Twain uses these three metaphors. Explain the literal meaning of these:

  "Throw off the bowlines": _____

  "Sail away from the safe harbor": _____

  "Catch the trade winds in your sails": _____

- What fears or circumstances sometimes hold you back from exploring, dreaming, and discovering?

  _____

  _____

- What things would you be MOST disappointed to have not done or tried in the next twenty years?

  _____

  _____

Mark Twain (1835–1910) *is a pen name for Samuel Clemens, a popular American writer and humorist. He was a careful observer of people and developed many memorable characters. Millions of kids and adults have enjoyed his novels, including* **The Adventures of Huckleberry Finn** *and* **The Adventures of Tom Sawyer**.

"I have learned to use the word 'impossible' with greatest caution."

– Wernher von Braun

● Before 1969, many people believed it would be impossible to ever land a human on the moon. But it happened on July 20, 1969, and the writer of this quote helped make it possible. What space accomplishments do you believe are possible in the future?

_____

_____

● "Paddling a stone canoe," from the *Iroquois Peacemaker Legend*, is a metaphor for doing the impossible. What "stone canoes" have you paddled successfully?

_____

_____

● Draw something that seems impossible but that you hope is possible.

Wernher von Braun (1912–1977) *was one of the world's leading rocket engineers and an authority on space travel. He helped develop the **Explorer** satellites, **Jupiter** rockets, **Pershing** and **Redstone** rockets, **Saturn** rockets and **Skylab**, and the world's first space station. He is most noted for directing the development of the **Saturn V** rocket that sent men to the moon for the first time. He also served as Director of NASA's Marshall Space Flight Center.*

" . . . hate in your heart will consume you too."

– Will Smith

● This quote is a line from Will Smith's rap, "Just the Two of Us." In the song, he gives advice about how to respond when people disrespect you and treat you badly. Do you agree that people should let go of hating others who mistreat them? (Explain your answer.)

_____

_____

● Describe a situation in your life where someone "made you mad, disrespected you, or treated you badly." Do not use real names.

_____

_____

_____

_____

● Do you think you can keep from having hate in your heart over situations like the one you described?

_____

Will Smith (1968–) *is a multitalented superstar. In the 1980s, fans knew the teenage Will as "The Fresh Prince of Bel-Air" from a hit TV show. Today, he is known as a movie star, rapper, and successful musician. He has had many hit movies, among them,* **Independence Day**, **Men in Black**, *and* **The Pursuit of Happyness***; and he has won several Grammy Awards.*

50

"Well begun is half done."

– Horace

SOMETIMES, WELL-BEGUN MEANS WELL-PAID, MR. HORACE.

Casius Construction

● Name something that you accomplished well partly due to a good beginning.

_____

_____

_____

_____

● Abraham Lincoln once said, "Give me six hours to chop down a tree and I will spend the first four sharpening the axe."

Compare Lincoln's statement to the quote by Horace:

_____

_____

_____

_____

Horace (Quintus Horatius Flaccus, 65–8 B.C.) _was the son of a freed slave in ancient Rome. He became one of the nation's greatest and most respected poets. His poems covered such topics as love, friendship, and beauty._

"One can never consent to creep when one feels the impulse to soar."

– Helen Keller

- Describe someone you know who is "creeping" through life, using excuses for not achieving. What "excuses" does the person use? (Do not use any real names.)

_____

_____

_____

Helen Keller and her teacher, Anne Sullivan

- In what situation or situations have you felt "an impulse to soar"?

_____

_____

_____

- Describe someone you know who has overcome financial, physical, or emotional handicaps and gone on to achieve success or satisfaction.

_____

_____

_____

Helen Keller (1880–1968) *became deaf and blind at the age of 19 months. A dedicated teacher taught her to communicate, and even though people often found it hard to understand her, she never gave up trying. She went to Radcliffe College, learned to read several foreign languages in Braille, wrote books and articles, gave speeches, and helped raise money for many organizations on behalf of blind people around the world.* **The Miracle Worker** *is a prize-winning drama based on her life and the work of her teacher, Anne Sullivan.*

Quotes to Start the Day

52

"Make sure you remember who you are, and all the stuff that made you laugh and dance and jump around. And in the dark times when, you know, stuff isn't going right, if you have something to hold on to, which is yourself, you'll survive it."

– Whoopi Goldberg

● In the "dark times," we sometimes take on others' opinions of ourselves. It is especially difficult to remember "who you are" when you are exposed to a lot of peer pressure. How do **you** manage to "hold on to yourself"?

_____

_____

_____

● Name some things that make you "laugh and dance and jump around."

_____

_____

_____

_____

Whoopi Goldberg (1950–) *was born Caryn Johnson in New York City and spent the first years of her life in a public housing project in Manhattan. After dropping out of high school, she worked as a camp counselor and performed in the choruses of several Broadway plays. Steven Spielberg cast her in the leading role in his film,* **The Color Purple***, which instantly established her as one of Hollywood's leading actresses. She went on to win an Academy Award, an Emmy, a Grammy, a Tony, Golden Globe Awards, People's Choice Awards, NAACP Image Awards, and Nickelodeon Kids' Choice Awards.*

58

53

"If you have a chance to accomplish something that will make things better for people coming behind you, and you don't do that, you are wasting your time on this Earth."

– Roberto Clemente

- Do you agree with Clemente's opinion? (Explain your answer.)

_____

_____

- What have **you** done that will make things better for people coming behind you?

_____

_____

_____

bob clemente

PITTSBURGH PIRATES
OUTFIELD

Roberto Clemente (1934–1972) _was a major league baseball player and a great hitter. Born in Puerto Rico, he served in the U.S. Marine Corps and played 18 seasons with the Pittsburgh Pirates. He won two World Series and a National League's Most Valuable Player award. During the off-season, he did charity work, often bringing food and baseball equipment to Latin American countries. While delivering aid to earthquake victims in 1972, he was killed in an airplane crash. After his death, he was inducted into the Baseball Hall of Fame._

- What could **you** do in the future to make sure you are not "wasting your time on this Earth"?

_____

_____

_____

_____

_____

_____

54

"You can't stay in your corner of the forest, waiting for others to come to you; you have to go to them sometimes."

– Winnie the Pooh

- When do you feel like "staying in your corner of the forest"?

  _____

  _____

- When do you wish others would come to you?

  _____

  _____

  _____

- How do you feel about "going out" to someone when you would rather they come to you?

  _____

  _____

Imagine taking advice from a teddy bear!

Winnie the Pooh *is a fictional bear created by English writer A. A. Milne in 1926. In the stories, Pooh lives in the Hundred Acre Wood and learns many life lessons with his friends Owl, Piglet, Tigger, Kanga, Eeyore, and Roo. The rights for merchandising the Pooh characters were licensed to Walt Disney in 1961, and several films and other animated productions have hit the theater and television screens. Pooh stuffed animals and other products have become a multimillion dollar business annually.*

· Volume One ·

Winnie-the-Pooh

Written by A. A. Milne

55

"Enthusiasm is everything."

– Pelé

● Get together with two or three other people. List some benefits of enthusiasm. Then make your own mini-poster promoting enthusiasm.

1._____

2._____

3._____

4._____

5._____

● Do you agree that enthusiasm is "everything"? If so, tell why. If not, tell what you think is needed instead of or in addition to enthusiasm.

_____

_____

_____

Pelé (1940–) *is known as "the world's greatest soccer player." Born Edison Arantes do Nascimento but known by his nickname, Pelé is a native of Brazil and a hero at home and abroad. He is the all-time top scorer of the Brazil National Football Team, and the only footballer (soccer player) to be on three World Cup winning teams. Since retirement, he has been a U.N. ambassador, a world ambassador for football (soccer), and a movie actor.*

Teacher Notes

Additional information or activities for each of the following quotes (by quote number):

1. Many quotes in this book, including this first one, will include metaphors or idioms. Review these concepts before using the Will Rogers quote.

2. As an optional activity (or instead of the final item on the page), challenge students to describe who they are in six words. Use the best-selling book titled *Six Word Memoirs* for examples and inspiration. See also **http://www.smithmag.net/sixwords**.

3. Students can find other quotes about reading or books, or can write their own aphorisms about books. Use this as a chance to transmit your own enthusiasm for reading, to help students become enchanted with books, and to discuss the concept of "classics" (books, movies, songs, cars) and how something—especially a book—comes to be called a classic.

4. As an extended activity, start with a group of situations (i.e., "what happened to someone"). Have students think of two or three different ways that someone might respond to each situation. Discuss as a group these responses in light of Mr. Holtz's statement.

5. Make sure students have some introduction to proverbs ahead of time. Let them try to explain what a proverb is and share any that they know.

6. This is a great opportunity to talk about dreams. Ask student to share their dreams (aspirations, imaginings). As an extended activity, students could write short "Why not?" poems.

7. Find proverbs from other cultures that give the same message as this quote.

8. Have students research James Barrie's story and the real-life children on which he built his characters in Peter Pan. Also, review the Peter Pan story. Students can look for evidence of Barrie's views about love in the story. If you wish to use this quote on Valentine's Day, look up the interesting history of Valentine's Day.

9. This quote can be a good springboard for a descriptive writing assignment.

10. Extend the goal-setting idea for middle-level students by having them make their own "senior yearbook page." They draw a picture of themselves and list their imagined/predicted high school accomplishments.

11. Students who have read Harry Potter books or seen the movies could give examples for the class of times in the book when a character stands up to a friend.

12. Have one group role-play a person losing his/her temper and another group role-play the same situation with a different response—a different way to handle the anger or the irritation (examples: traffic, long line at the store, someone interrupting them when they speak, perceived unfair treatment, etc.).

13. This is a good activity for perspective: Students could fill in the quote as themselves, then as someone they know, then as a famous or historical figure, or as a person in another country, etc.

14. Students might have fun brainstorming all the things they can name that require waiting.

15. This quote works well when explaining reading strategies and the need to anticipate, preview, and predict before reading. Students can discuss other situations in which this quote holds true.

16. Review the concept of hyperbole before introducing this quote.

17. Students could discuss the difference between expecting things of yourself and operating out of the expectations of others. (For example: How do these differ in the results? How do these differ in the way you feel about yourself?)

18. Review the idea that the "falling" metaphor is often used to describe failure. Also, students will find it interesting to know that Michael Jordan (quoted on this page) was cut from the sophomore high school basketball team because he was not tall enough (at 5 ft 11 inches).

Additional information or activities for each of the following quotes (by quote number):

19. This quote can lead to a good discussion on the topic of metaphors and symbolism. Candles, flame, light, and heat, for instance, mean a variety of things throughout literature.

20. Students can role-play a situation as a cynical, grumpy person might confront it. Then role-play the same situation as a hopeful person might confront it. Compare and contrast the outcomes.

21. This quote is illustrated in a literal way in the Cinderella story; only one person can fit into the glass slipper and, therefore, into the prince's life. Use this idea to expand the discussion of the quote.

22. Students will enjoy making up their own situations that can be viewed by a pessimist or an optimist.

23. Before introducing this quote, define and discuss "character" and give examples. Also have students define "integrity."

24. As a worthwhile research extension, have students interview people whom they believe are "successful in life." They can ask those people to explain what made them successful.

25. Students can try writing bits of advice that use the same kind of play on similar-sounding words.

26. There are several excellent online resources for learning more about Anne Frank, including **www.ushmm.org** (United States Holocaust Memorial Museum site) and **www.annefrank.org**.

27. The work and writings of Benjamin Franklin make an excellent topic for an interdisciplinary unit incorporating U.S. history, science, math, and literature.

28. Talk about "voice" and what it means to have and use your own.

29. A good extension of this quote would be to rewrite the metaphor using a more modern example. For instance, instead of a "coat of mail," what could students think of that couldn't be pierced? Discuss this question: "How does the timeliness of the metaphor affect its impact?"

30. A good follow-up activity would be to have students set a goal to try something they think they can't do, then report back (or write) about their experience.

31. As an extension, students can research other Native American music or any music projects or songs that were specifically designed as a healing force.

32. Write some group proverbs about the tongue—in the spirit of these proverbs.

33. Here's another quote by Henry Van Dyke to discuss: "Time is: Too slow for those who wait, too swift for those who fear."

34. Find out about the instrument Hipparchus is holding in the illustration (which is an old wood block print). Learn its name and its use.

35. Extend these activities by having students write comparisons between humans and other animals.

36. Students can draw cartoons to illustrate the advice in this quote.

37. After reading the quote, but before students do the task on the page, do one together. Give an example of a mistake that they can recognize. As a group, brainstorm different responses that could be made to that mistake.

38. This proverb is an excellent start for a discussion about peer pressure and about those who support each other's negative behavior.

39. Use this quote to illustrate and discuss the concept of irony.

40. Extend the simile activity by having students start similes and pass them to peers to complete.

41. Many Yogi-isms make wonderful discussion starters. They can be found at **www.yogiberra.com**.

42. Extend the activity by having students work in pairs to write their own aphorisms about luck.

43. Work as a whole class to make a list of ten alternatives to blaming someone else when one fails (i.e., "What are some healthy or positive ways to respond when you fail?"). Students can set a goal to practice these alternatives.

44. The fable, *The Little Prince*, makes several profound observations. You might read excerpts from the book to students.

45. Share favorite personal stories about being late.

Additional information or activities for each of the following quotes (by quote number):

46. This is a good quote to kick off a unit on community service or volunteerism.

47. Mark Twain is an excellent subject for an interdisciplinary unit—tying in history, literature, and science (specifically rivers and waterways). Tell students about Twain's background and history with the river (thus explaining the metaphors). Research the meaning of his pen name, "Mark Twain."

48. NASA's web site, **www.nasa.gov**, is an excellent resource for both historical and modern aerospace innovations.

49. Look up the entire lyrics for Will Smith's rap, "Just the Two of Us." Discuss who the speaker is and who the listener is in this song. Extend the activity to write two lines of a rap on a specific topic. A wider group can decide how to combine these lines into a longer, cohesive rap.

50. This quote is an excellent springboard for teaching introductory sentences and paragraphs in students' writing.

51. There are many wonderful teaching materials about Helen Keller available online at **http://gardenofpraise.com/ibdkell.htm**.

52. There are many stories and articles about people who have held onto something in themselves to survive difficult times, including captivity and persecution. Think of and share at least one such story with students. This quote also ties well to Anne Frank's outlook during her time in hiding, illustrated in a quote #26.

53. Use this quote as a part of a kickoff for a unit or lesson on human interdependence or on environmentalism and conservation.

54. Many of the Pooh stories have characters and themes that relate to people of all ages; they provide excellent, easy-to-understand illustrations of these important life insights.

55. There is often a direct correlation between enthusiasm and success, whether in business, education, entertainment, or sports. As a follow-up activity, students could interview people they admire, and ask what they are enthusiastic about and why.